796.5

X

A & C BLACK

Published by:
A & C Black Publishers Limited
36 Soho Square
London W1D 3QY

www.acblack.com

First published 2011
Copyright © 2011 A & C Black Publishers
Limited

Original concept: Paul Mason
Project management: Paul Mason
Design: Mayer Media

ISBN   HB 9781408142424
          PB 9781408142431

This book is produced using paper made from
wood grown in managed, sustainable forests.
It is natural, renewable, and recyclable. The
logging and manufacturing processes conform
to the environmental regulations of the
country of origin.

Printed and bound in Malaysia by
Tien Wah Press

WARNING!
**Some of the skills described in this book
are dangerous, or can lead to dangerous
situations if performed incorrectly. Only
undertake them when you are 100%
confident you can do so safely.**

Photo acknowledgements
All interior photos supplied by *Bushcraft and
Survival Skills* magazine, except pages 24 (left,
main), 27 (left), 28 (right) all Paul Mason.

Cover photos: Shutterstock

Where appropriate, every effort has been
made to contact copyright holders of material
reproduced in this book. Any omissions will
be rectified in subsequent editions if the
publisher is given notice.

Contents

Why become a
survival skills expert?

Want to be the next Bear Grylls? Ever wondered how to signal for help, or catch a fish with your bare hands? If you found yourself lost and alone, thirsty, hungry and cold, could you survive? Could you light a fire without a match, for example? If you want to learn what it takes to survive in the wilds, this book shows you how!

ANNOY YOUR FRIENDS BY HELPING THEM
Not only will you be able to enjoy and explore the outdoors with greater confidence, discovering all that nature provides. You'll also be able to guide your friends along the way, keeping them out of danger during your adventures. And who knows, one day you may even use your expert skills to save someone's life!

SAVE CASH!
Companies spend thousands of pounds developing the latest and safest piece of survival kit. But we'll show you how, with just a few items and the correct knowledge, you can create your own kit, saving you lots of cash in the process.

FYI!
These features are scattered throughout the book. They contain information you can casually drop into conversation to amaze, astound, and impress your friends.

Start a fire without a match, using tree bark! See pages 10-13 to find out how.

Want to know how to send a
distress signal? See page 30.

EVERY KIND OF SURVIVAL SITUATION

Whatever kind of survival situation you find
yourself in, you will find this book is crammed
with helpful information. From building a
shelter to making a fire in the wilderness,
finding water, or tracking wild animals, there's
information on just about everything you
might need to know to survive.

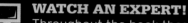

WATCH AN EXPERT!

Throughout the book these panels
point you towards web pages where you
can see the relevant skills being put into
practice.

Use your hat to pick stinging
nettles. See page 7 for more
innovative uses for your hat!

SURVIVAL KIT

The basic survival kit you will
need is listed on pages 8 and 9.
Some challenges also require
specialist kit, which is listed in panels
like this one.

LOST FOR WORDS

look here for explanations of
those tricky, technical words

Clothing for the **wilds**

The first rule of survival is to protect yourself from the weather. There is no point finding water or building a shelter if you get hypothermia **or heat stroke in the process! Your clothes can protect you from heat, cold, and wet. They can also keep you safe from stinging plants, insects and thorns.**

LAYER UP!

The secret to dressing for the outdoors is to wear layers. Between each layer of clothing the air warms up, keeping you warm in cold weather. If you are too warm, you can remove a layer. Adjust your layers, aiming to sweat as little - and stay as dry - as possible.

MID LAYER

This layer keeps you warm. Wear a fabric that will **wick** away moisture and let your skin breathe. A woolly jumper with a hood or high neckline will stop the neck area from losing heat. A cotton shirt may be enough to keep you warm when worn over a base layer, depending on the climate.

OUTER LAYER

An outer layer of a good waterproof jacket and trousers will protect you from wind and rain. The jacket should have a hood with a peak, and adjustable drawstrings to keep the hood snug. A long tail will keep your bottom dry when you sit down! For the trousers, tight ankles keep insects out.

BASE LAYER

The base layer is worn next to your skin: it needs to be warm, comfortable and dry. There are two main kinds, synthetic thermals and soft **merino** wool. Merino can be worn for long periods without smelling - you might as well survive and smell good too!

If you learn one thing from this section, make it:
• **Wear layers**

hypothermia lowered body temperature: the most severe cases of hypothermia can lead to death
wick draw away moisture
merino breed of sheep with very soft wool

BOOTS AND SOCKS

Choose a pair of comfortable, waterproof hiking boots. If they cover the ankle, this adds support, and keeps your feet dry in puddles. Socks made of natural fibres, with padded heels and toes, are best.

HAT

In cold weather, a hat will stop heat loss from your head. If it is warm and sunny, a hat protects you from heatstroke or sunburn.

FYI!

Aim for your outdoor clothing to be suitable for staying out all night in a storm and still remaining relatively comfortable!

SECRET TRICK

Hats come in handy in all sorts of survival situations.

1 Use your hat as an improvised glove to collect stinging nettles, or perhaps to keep insects at bay.

2 If your hat is waterproof, you could use it to collect water. If it is not waterproof, you can instead use your hat to filter water before you purify it. (See page 20 for ways to purify water.)

Kit for the wilds

Your survival kit will be invaluable if you find yourself in an emergency situation. It includes essential survival materials. When choosing what to take, consider the weight, size and function of each thing. Items that are simple, compact and serve several purposes are ideal. Remember, you have to carry everything in your pack!

CARRYING YOUR KIT

Carry your survival kit in a rucksack. Line the rucksack with a heavy-duty waterproof bag, and place all your kit inside the bag to keep it dry. The bag can also be used for collecting water, building a shelter, keeping you warm and dry and (if you choose a bright colour) as a way of signalling for help.

SURVIVAL KIT CONTENTS

The photos show some of the things that a survival expert would be likely to carry in their rucksack. The names of each bit of kit, running from left to right, top to bottom, are shown in the panel.

- Folding multi-tool
- Torch
- Survival bag
- Whistle
- **Fire steel** or matches
- **Tinder** kit
- Mobile phone
- Cord
- Compass
- Small first-aid kit
- Plastic food bag
- Rations

> If you learn one thing from this section:
> • **Pack only the things you really need**

> **fire steel** stick of metal that creates a shower of sparks when scraped
> **tinder** material used for starting a fire
> **spork** eating tool combining spoon, fork and knife in one

SURVIVING DISASTERS

Your survival kit could also be useful when you are not in the wilds. Having it handy means you will have a better chance of surviving a disaster such as a tsunami, earthquake, flood, or accident. The kit's supplies of food, water purification equipment, first-aid, clothing and tools would each come in useful in a post-disaster situation.

SECRET TRICK

Seal the ends of your matches in wax to make them waterproof. That way if they get wet you will still be able to light a fire!

1 Light a candle in a container that you'll be able to tilt, to get at the melted wax without burning yourself.

2 Tip the container to the side and dip the match heads one by one into the wax. Be careful not to light any accidentally! Once the wax dries, repeat if necessary: you will be left with waterproof matches.

• **Spork**
• **Small cooking pot**

• **Water bottle**
• **Water purification tablets**

FYI!

We sweat out 250ml of moisture per hour when walking, and 350ml when carrying a heavy load such as a backpack. That's why drinking water is so important for survival.

Preparing a fire

Fire will dry your clothes, keep you warm, provide light, signal for help, heat food and drive away insects. Being able to start a fire and keep the fire going is an essential survival skill. (When practising these skills, check that the area you are in allows open fires.)

Your preparation materials will include:
• **Dry tinder from your survival kit or surroundings**
• Kindling: **twigs the thickness of**
1) **matchsticks**
2) **pencils**
3) **your thumb**
• **Fuel: sticks and branches up to the thickness of your wrist**

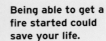

Being able to get a fire started could save your life.

COLLECTING MATERIALS
Look for tinder, kindling and fuel that are dead and as dry as possible. Dry twigs and branches will snap when you break them. **Green wood** contains a lot of water, so it does not burn well. The best place to find dry fuel is off the ground. Broken branches lodged in trees or shrubs will be **seasoned**. Dead wood found on the ground, on the other hand, may have absorbed moisture: it will still burn, but not as well as dead wood found off the ground.

KEEP TINDER AND FUEL DRY
Lay out the plastic liner from your rucksack, or a waterproof coat or sheet. Put the tinder and fuel on it as you collect it so that it stays dry. Lay it out in the order you are going to use it: tinder, kindling, and larger pieces of wood.

> **green wood** living or recently cut wood, which is damp inside
>
> **kindling** material that burns easily and can be used when starting a fire
>
> **seasoned** wood without internal moisture, which is dry and burns well

Once everything is to hand, you will be ready to light your tinder and get the fire going.

CONSTRUCT THE FIRE

Look for a level and dry area, with no overhanging branches or foliage that could catch light. Lay some twigs next to each other to form a platform: this protects your tinder from the damp ground. Place a bundle of tinder loosely on top of the platform, and add two bundles of the thinnest kindling (propped against a log to allow oxygen flow).

SECRET TRICK

You can use toilet roll, cotton wool, or paper as tinder. But what if you don't have any of those?

1 Dried grass or dead pine needles make good tinder. The best tinder is probably birch bark, which contains flammable oils.

2 You will see birch bark peeling off birch trees. Collect this whenever you see it and store it somewhere dry. (Only ever peel off bark that is naturally coming away and peels off easily, or you will damage the tree.)

FYI!

Always know the local laws and seek the landowner's permission before starting a fire – unless your life is at risk, of course!

11

Now **light** a **fire**

Your fire-lighting materials could include:
- **fire steel**
- **cord for making a bow (see Secret Trick panel)**

Three vital ingredients are needed for your fire: fuel, oxygen and heat. Without each of these, the fire will fail. Success could mean something as simple as fanning the fire to give it more oxygen, or correctly positioning your kindling so that it is in the hottest part of the flame.

FYI!

The sparks from a fire steel burn at 3000 °C. Wow – that's hot!

SPARK UP YOUR FIRE
Grip the fire steel with one hand, and with the other hand hold the striker at the top of the fire steel. Scrape the striker firmly and slowly down the fire steel at an angle of 45 degrees, to create a fountain of sparks. Repeat until the tinder lights.

Watch our expert light a fire out in the wilderness, using only simple materials! Check out the action at:
www.acblack.com/instantexpert

notch V-shaped cut on the surface of something

ADD KINDLING
With your tinder alight, gently place a handful of kindling on top of your fire. You might need to place a log beside your tinder, so that the twigs are raised and airflow is maintained. As these catch light, place the pencil-thick sticks on the fire. Once these are burning, add the finger-thick sticks. Finally, add the thicker sticks. (See pages 36 and 37 for information on having a fire and leaving no trace.)

WARNING!
Fire is dangerous. Do not undertake any of these activities unless you are 100% confident you can do so safely.

SECRET TRICK
If you don't have a fire steel, you can start a fire using a bow drill.

1 As above, you need a bow, a sharpened stick with domed end, a notched piece of wood, and a baseboard with a **notch**.

2 Loop the bowstring around the sharpened drill stick, and put the ends into the notches. Saw back and forth with increasing speed and downwards pressure. Dark powder will start to fill the notch. Stop when this is smoking on its own.

3 Fan the powder until it glows. Place it in a tinder bundle and blow it into flame.

Bear Grylls survival expert

Bear Grylls is an internationally famous survival expert. He regularly appears on TV, taking on some of the world's toughest challenges and introducing survival techniques to other people. Today, Bear works as an author, presenter, and star of the Discovery Channel series *Man V Wild* and *Born Survivor*.

LEARNING ABOUT SURVIVAL

Bear's work shows people how it's possible to survive in some of the world's most beautiful yet hostile environments:

"Learning to look after yourself and be able to survive in the great outdoors gives us a great sense of pride. It is a very natural urge to want to explore and live wild. Done well, it brings out the true person in us that is real, raw, strong and calm. Understanding nature reconnects us to a part of us that goes way, way back."

As a result of his work to teach survival skills, Bear has been appointed as the Chief Scout for the Scouting Association.

Bear takes part in a photo shoot, wearing an outdoor jacket he helped to design.

Bear first became famous as a climber when he became the youngest person ever to climb Mount Everest.

Bear takes his role as Chief Scout seriously. Here he offers encouragement to other members of the Scouting Association.

FUN FACTS

Real Name: Edward Grylls (Edward became Teddy, then Teddy Bear, then Bear – which stuck).

Birthday: 7 June 1974.

Height: 6ft (183 cm).

Key quote: "The real heart of survival is motivation; it is the drive to keep going, the determination to see it through, whatever the pain, the discomfort, or the cost."

First TV appearance: On a 'Sure for Men' deodorant commercial in 2005.

Worst things he has eaten: Elephant dung, frozen yak eyeballs, raw alligator brain.

Scariest moment: Jumping off a raft and unintentionally landing on a tiger shark!

Most feared animal: The saltwater crocodile – they have been known to grab a human off a yacht that's out of sight of the shore!

Favourite bit of survival kit: "The brain is our best tool! It can think imaginatively, help drive us, and make smart, fast, instinctive decisions at important moments."

BEAR'S BACKGROUND

Bear first became famous when he climbed Mount Everest at the age of 23. At the time this made him the youngest person to have climbed the world's tallest mountain. He is a former soldier, and served in Britain's elite SAS regiment as a trooper, patrol medic, and survival instructor.

FYI!

If Bear Grylls could teach one survival skill, his advice would be: "Never, ever, ever give up. This is the greatest survival lesson. End of story."

Shelter building for **survival**

Imagine if you needed to get away from the elements, or hide from the creatures of the night. Making a shelter that kept you dry and safe would be a survival skill you would be thankful for. Take your time, and decide what kind of shelter you need. Rushed shelters are usually fragile and leaky!

If there is plenty of fallen wood, you can build a great debris shelter (see pages 18 and 19) without tools or cord. Otherwise you will need:
- **multi-tool with a saw**
- **cord**

If you are in a group, working together will mean the shelter can be built much more quickly. Just make sure it's big enough for everyone!

THINGS TO BEAR IN MIND
Ask yourself some key questions before deciding what kind of shelter you should be building. These will help you decide whether it needs to be a quickly built shelter, or something more solid:

· What's the shelter for?
If it's for shade during a single day, a fast shelter will do. If it may have to last for several days in wind and rain, you will need to spend more time building it.

· What materials are available?
Do you have anything with you to help build your shelter, such as string or plastic sheeting? What other resources are there around: for example, branches, bracken and leaf litter.

· How much time do you have?
You do not want to be left in the dark with only half of your shelter built! (Bear in mind that it gets darker much sooner in thick woodland.)

hazard potential danger; something that could go wrong in the future

CHECK FOR HAZARDS

You might think that you have picked the perfect spot, but there are loads of potential **hazards** to consider. Check the surrounding area for streams that could flood, and signs that animals use the area. Look up to check for broken branches or places rocks could fall down from. There is no point building a lovely survival shelter, then finding a great big branch lands on you in the middle of the night!

Watch our expert build a shelter in the wilderness, using only simple materials! Check out the action at: **www.acblack.com/instantexpert**

SECRET TRICK

You can save time and effort by using a natural structure as part of your shelter.

1 Caves or dense vegetation (for example, underneath a low-hanging, thick fir tree) may provide a ready-made shelter.

2 Rock faces, the walls of old abandoned buildings, and even the roots of an upturned tree will shield you from the wind, and could be used as a wall for your shelter.

17

Build a debris shelter

To make a debris shelter you need:
- **straight pole 2.5m/8'2" long**
- **two 0.5m/ 1'8" poles**
- **cord**
- **leaves, sticks and other forest-floor debris**

In woodland there will almost certainly be plenty of dead leaves and branches lying around. This material can be used to build a debris shelter: these make an ideal small, short-term shelter. Debris shelters are so well insulated **that a well-built one can keep you warm in temperatures below freezing.**

insulated wrapped up to stop heat escaping

MAKE THE FRAME

Rope together the two short poles to form an X, with much shorter arms at the top than the bottom. Now rest the long pole into the top of the X, and rest the other end on the ground to make a stretched-out pyramid shape. Place branches from the ground to the long pole along each side to make walls. The branches need to be as close as possible, and must not come up higher than the ridge pole or your shelter will leak.

FILL IN ANY GAPS, AND COVER

Fill gaps in the walls with thinner sticks, or lay on bracken or spreading branches with leaves or needles on them. This adds extra strength and insulation, and stops any debris falling through while you are snoring! Cover the branches with an arm's length thickness of debris.

PREPARE YOUR MATTRESS

Fill the inside with the driest, comfiest debris you can find. The less space there is around you, the warmer your shelter will be. Leave just enough room for an entrance so that you can shuffle inside backwards. Prepare for a lovely night's sleep!

SECRET TRICK

Stop your candle falling over, using a natural candlestick. You need a branch, plus a strip of peeled bark and some string or long grass (each about as long as your hand).

1 Make a split at the top of the stick, then put the two ends of the bark together and slide them into the split. Put your candle into the loop formed and pull the tab tight.

2 Bind the top of the branch together with your string or grass, and the candle should be held tightly in place.

FYI!

Remember to go to the toilet before you climb inside your debris shelter! It takes a while to wriggle in and out, so you don't want to have to get up in the night...

Water collection
and **safety**

In a survival situation, you must have water or you will die within days. But what if there is no stream or river in the area? Fortunately, there is a way of plucking water literally out of thin air, night or day. What you need is a vegetation still.

FYI!
Humans can only live 3 days, *maximum*, without water!

Water from a stream like this one will need to be purified before it is definitely safe to drink.

To make a vegetation still you will need:
- **clear, hole-free plastic bag**
- **some vegetation**

FIND SOME VEGETATION
First, find some vegetation. You need a leafy plant that will fit plenty of foliage inside your plastic bag. Place the bag over a branch, fitting in as many leaves as you can. Make sure you pick a branch that's sturdy enough to take the weight of water filling the bag.

SEAL THE BAG
Position a corner of the plastic bag so that it hangs down lower than any other part. Next, seal the opening of the bag around the branch using string, cord or tape from your survival kit. You need an airtight seal, but make sure it is not so tight that it kills the branch. Make sure there is plenty of air in the bag, so that it balloons out rather than hanging limply.

vegetation still device for turning condensation into drinking water

WAIT... THEN COLLECT YOUR WATER!

Now you have to be patient. Leave the bag for 4-6 hours. When you return there should be roughly a cupful of water in the bag. How much water you get depends partly on the time of day and weather conditions. A vegetation still left in the sunshine all afternoon will produce the most water.

WATER PURIFICATION

The water you drink must be clean and safe to drink, or you will become ill. A safe method of purifying water from a stream or lake is to boil it. Bring the water to a fierce boil for at least 5 minutes, ideally more. Alternatively you can use purification tablets, often included in survival kits, though these may give the water a strange chemical taste.

FYI!

When making a vegetation still, avoid using poisonous plants or plants with waxy leaves.

SECRET TRICK

A 'survival straw' is a great way to purify water that you think might be dangerous to drink. They are small enough to slip into your coat pocket, and safe to use anywhere.

1 You dip the straw into dirty water, and suck hard to pull the liquid through. A filter inside the straw gets rid of impurities.

2 Some survival straws will process 500 litres of water, which is 5 glasses a day for a year. That's an awful lot of sucking!

Make **your** own survival tin

A survival tin is a compact, lightweight tin containing key items for survival. With one of these in your pack, you are prepared for most situations. You can buy ready-made survival tins quite cheaply, or make up your own.

WHAT DO YOU PUT IN YOUR TIN?
The advantage of making up your own survival tin is that you get to include items according to the kind of area you are visiting.

Needle and thread: for repairs, removing splinters and making an improvised compass.

Flexible saw: for cutting branches.

Mini fire steel: can be used to start a fire even when wet.

Waterproof matches: carry a few in your survival tin (to be used only when other fire-lighting methods fail!)

Candle: a great source of light and useful for starting a fire. Shave two sides flat so that it fits in your tin.

Fishhooks and line: a few small hooks, split lead weights and plenty of line. (Remember, a small hook can catch a large or small fish, but a large hook can only catch a large fish!)

Mini compass: navigating with a compass is tricky – if you don't know how, don't include this! (See page 26 to learn more about compass navigation.)

SECRET TRICK

Using a shiny surface to reflect the sunlight is a way of sending a distress signal. This takes a bit of practice, as you need to aim the reflected light accurately.

1 Anything shiny will do - including the lid of your survival tin. If it needs a polish, use a bit of toothpaste!

2 Once the lid is nice and shiny, you can use it to reflect sunlight and signal for help. (See page 30 for more information on signalling.)

Cotton wool: good tinder that can be squashed into your tin.

Emergency blanket: for warmth and shelter.

Whistle: to attract attention.

Small torch: for light and signalling.

OTHER USEFUL THINGS

Purification tablets or survival straw: to make water safe to drink.

Energy tablets: emergency energy source.

Insulating tape: tape this around the outside of the tin to make it waterproof. The tape might come in handy later, too!

 deterioration getting progressively worse

Tracking wild animals

Learning to track an animal successfully might lead you to your next meal, or to a water supply. Tracking is also a great hobby. You can follow animal tracks, identify the creature that made them, and find out what they eat, where they sleep and how they play. So, how do you work out if there are animals around?

When tracking animals, you might find it useful to have:
• **small binoculars/a monocular**

Identifying tracks is much easier in snow, but they are also easy to spot in wet or muddy areas.

LOOK FOR TRAILS

Animal trails usually go to where animals eat, drink and shelter. A trail may be used by more than one species, so you may find a variety of different tracks on the same trail. Now take a closer look. Along the trail you are likely to find **scat**. Scat is a polite way of saying animal poo. Is it fresh, warm, smelly? That will tell you how long ago the animal was here.

IDENTIFY SLEEPING AREAS

Many animals return to or leave their sleeping area at sunrise or dusk, so these are good times to try and spot them. Some animals sleep underground, so look for openings in the ground. Larger openings will be home to bigger animals: badger holes are much more impressive than those made by rabbits, for example. Other animals, such as hare and deer, sleep in the open. Their sleeping area is likely to be a flattened area that has a similar shape to their body.

> **scat** animal excrement or poo

SECRET TRICK

Take a cast of animal footprints, as a way of recording animal evidence to show your friends. You will need plaster of Paris, an old toothbrush, a strip of card and a paper clip.

1 Place the strip of card in a circular shape around the print and clip it together. Then mix the plaster of Paris and pour it inside.

LOOK FOR OTHER CLUES

Other clues that there could be animals around include:
• damaged bark or branches on trees, and exposed roots along the trail. This will likely have been caused by animals eating the bark or rubbing against it
• tooth marks in nutshell remains
• fur caught on bushes or barbed wire.

2 Once the plaster is completely hard, carefully remove the strip of card and gently use the toothbrush to remove any soil or debris. There you have it – one animal print!

FYI!

If you soak an owl's pellet in water for a while, you can carefully take it apart using tweezers. You will be amazed at what's inside!

Never get lost

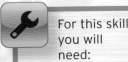

For this skill you will need:
- **compass**
- **map**

Before you set off on an expedition, it is a good idea to know how to read a map and use a compass. Once you can use a map to understand the area and terrain, you will find it easier to locate water and pick the best spot to make camp. And of course, you will also find it easier to avoid getting lost!

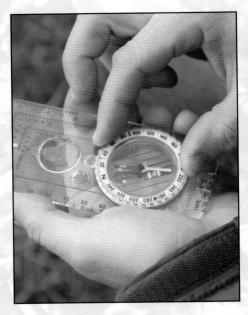

GET FAMILIAR WITH YOUR COMPASS

Almost all compasses have a dial you can turn so that the needle is pointing at north on the dial, while the base is pointing in a different direction. Once you have the needle and 'north' markings aligned, you can also see which directions are south, east and west.

ORIENTATE YOUR MAP

First, align your map visually with the terrain around you, using features such as hills, lakes, buildings or woods. Then place your compass on the map so that the long edge of the base plate connects your starting point with your destination. Hold the map and compass in place, and turn the compass dial until north-south on the dial lines up with north-south on the map.

bearing the direction you need to travel
terrain the physical features of the ground or land

SECRET TRICK

If you don't have a compass with you, it's possible to make a very rough one using a needle from your survival tin.

Following rivers or streams can be a good way to find your route, as long as you can see on a map that they go in the right direction.

1 Repeatedly stroke the needle against your hair in one direction (take care not to hurt yourself!). This will eventually make it magnetic.

FINDING YOUR BEARING

Rotate the map and compass together until the north needle aligns with the north arrow on the dial. The compass base will now be pointing off in a different direction. This is your **bearing**. Before you move off in that direction, look ahead and choose a landmark such as a rock or tree to walk towards. When you have reached this, repeat the whole process.

FYI!

There is more than one north! True north is found using sun or star readings. Grid north is north on a map. Magnetic north is where a compass needle points.

2 Lay the magnetized needle on a piece of paper, a blade of grass, a leaf or a piece of thin bark floating in some water. The needle will gently float around until it points north. (See page 28 for other ways of finding north.)

Use nature to **navigate**

If you are stranded or lost without a map and a compass, don't panic. (In fact, NEVER panic in a survival situation.) Have a look around you: if you know what to look for, there are all kinds of natural signposts that will help you find your way.

> **!** There are no special tools needed for this skill. Just:
> • **keep your eyes peeled for nature's navigational signs!**

WIND-BLOWN TREES

It's always worth checking which direction the wind usually blows in the area you're exploring. The branches of windswept trees will always point away from wind. This means exposed trees can give you clues about navigation and direction.

MOSSES AND LICHENS

Look out for moss and lichen. It usually grows on the side of a rock or tree that the sun shines the least. Where the growth is thickest will be north in the **northern hemisphere** and south in the **southern hemisphere**. Watch out, though – if the trees or rocks are very shaded this won't work, because not enough sunlight will be getting through.

CRESCENT MOON

If there is a crescent moon, draw an invisible line between the two horns of the moon to the horizon. The point where the line hits the horizon will be roughly south in the northern hemisphere and north in the southern hemisphere. This technique is not completely accurate, but gives a rough direction.

THE SUN
The sun rises approximately in the east and sets approximately in the west. At midday it is positioned due north in the southern hemisphere and due south in the northern hemisphere.

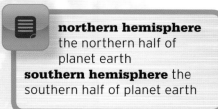

northern hemisphere the northern half of planet earth
southern hemisphere the southern half of planet earth

SECRET TRICK
On a bright day, you can use this simple trick with a stick and a pair of stones to work out north-south and east-west lines:

1 Push a straight stick into level ground, so that the stick is pointing as upright as possible. Place a stone at the end of the stick's shadow. This stone represents west.

2 Wait for three hours. The end of the stick's shadow will have moved. Place another stone at the new location, which represents east.

3 Use a stick or cord to make a line between the two stones, as in the photo. This now runs in an east-west direction.

4 Draw a line from the stick directly between the two stones. This line points north.

SOS

In a survival situation you may need to signal for help. There are lots of different ways of getting attention and attracting rescuers, using either sound or sight. If you are able to, signal from open or high ground where you can be seen. If you move about, try to leave signs to tell rescuers where you have gone.

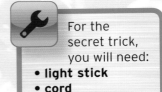

For the secret trick, you will need:
- **light stick**
- **cord**

MOBILE PHONE

If there is power in the phone and you have a signal, this is the best way to call for help. Even if you can't call, you may still be able to send a text message. Always store the number for the relevant rescue service in your phone before you set out. If you have forgotten to do this, call a reliable friend instead. They can summon help on your behalf.

BUILD A SIGNAL FIRE

A flaming, smoking fire will attract attention. You can prepare a fire following the instructions on pages 10 and 11. If you don't have enough fuel to keep a fire going, get the fire prepared and keep it dry, so that it's ready to light when you hear a vehicle of some sort coming. (Always make sure a fire is properly put out before leaving the site.)

THREE IS THE MAGIC NUMBER!

Doing something three times is recognized as meaning that the signaler is in difficulty and needs help. To send a distress signal with a whistle, for example, give three sharp blasts on the whistle, pause, and repeat at regular intervals. To signal with a torch, click the torch on for a count of three, then off for another count of three. Repeat twice more, making a total of (you guessed it) three flashes.

FYI!

When signalling for help using a mirrored surface, signal in flashes. This will attract more attention, and avoid dazzling your rescuers!

SECRET TRICK

The bigger your signal, the more chance you have of being spotted. This trick is a great way to make a light stick seem much bigger than it really is.

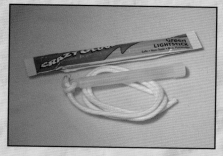

1 Fix about an arm's length of cord through the hole in the end of a light stick.

2 Crack the light stick to activate it, and swing it round on the end of the cord. It works like a sparkler being twirled around, making a big circle of light that will attract attention at night.

Survival **fishing**

Fish contain most of the vitamins that our bodies need for survival. If you are near a river, a lake or the ocean, you will be able to use the fishing kit from your survival tin (see page 22) to catch your dinner. Even if you don't have a whole fishing kit, never despair. There may be other things around that you can use.

In a river such as this there will almost certainly be fish. Catching them may take a lot of patience – but it could keep you alive!

It's possible to use large buds, such as these rosehips, as a float when fishing in the wilderness.

HOOKS

If you have something to use as line, you can make a fish hook from any bit of wire or a safety pin, for example. Alternatively, you can use a shaped splinter of wood or bone to create a **gorge hook**, which turns like a toggle in the fish's throat after it has swallowed the bait. If you are near the sea, you can use feathers tied to a small gorge hook to catch mackerel.

LINE

Line is very tricky to make from scratch in the wild, though it is possible. But think for a moment about whether you already have some. Is there a draw-cord in your jacket that could be split and used as a short line, for example? Or could you use your bootlaces?

SECRET TRICK

If you don't have any fishing kit, but can see trout in the stream, try tickling one out of the water:

1 Put your hand in the water and let it adjust to the temperature. Then wade gently towards the fish from behind.

If you manage to catch a trout, it will taste great roasted over a fire.

2 Gently slide your hands underneath the fish, lightly wiggling your fingers to imitate the flow of the water. Once your hand is in position, quickly scoop the fish out of the water onto the bank.

BAIT

You can usually find a worm by lifting a log or rock, particularly in a damp, shady area. Or try a slug, maggot, beetle or grasshopper as bait. Fish will also bite fruit and nuts. Finally, try pulling something shiny or a feather quickly through the water to see if a fish is curious enough to bite on it.

FYI!

You can eat any freshwater fish that's shorter than your finger raw, without boning or gutting it.

gorge hook type of fish hook that catches in the fish's throat

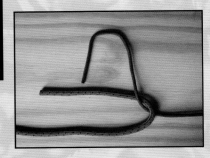

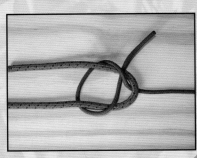

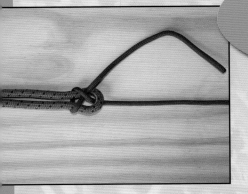

Get knotted!

Knowing a few knots could not only save your life, but also make things much more comfortable in a survival situation. You will need to use knots when shelter building, fishing, setting up your camp, in first aid, and perhaps even for climbing down a cliff or rescuing a friend from the water.

SHEET BEND

A sheet bend is a good knot to use if you want to join two ropes together. If the ropes are different sizes, always use the larger rope to form the starting loop, as shown in the photos. To tie a sheet bend:

1) Form a loop in one rope and hold it in one hand.

2) Pass the thinner piece of rope through the loop, then around the loop.

3) Take care to go round the short **working end** first, then the long end.

4) Finally, tuck the smaller rope back under itself, and pull tight to finish the knot.

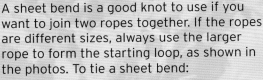

FYI!

Knots, twists and kinks weaken your rope. Research shows that tying a knot in a rope can weaken it by 20–50%.

diameter distance across a circle at its widest point
working end end of a rope used to tie a knot

All you need to practise tying knots is:

- **cord or rope, ideally two pieces of different** diameter

SECRET TRICK

To give yourself a visual reminder of the key knots you want to remember, why not make a knot board?

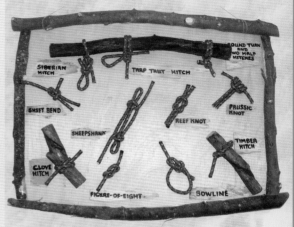

1 First, tie your favourite, most useful knots out of similar-sized cord. (If you use different colours for the two sides of each knot, it will be easier to see how it is tied.)

2 Then pin or glue your knots to a board, or even sew them to a piece of cloth, such as an old tea towel. That way, you can roll up your knots and take them with you.

TIMBER HITCH

A timber hitch is a useful knot if you are using a rope to drag firewood or branches. The more strain you put on this knot, the tighter it gets – but it is always easy to untie. To tie a timber hitch:

1) Pass the end of the rope around your bundle of wood (in the photos, the stick takes the place of the wood), leaving a long working end.

2) Pass the end over the rope, then tuck it through the loop you made around the wood. Wrap the end of the rope around the loop 3 times.

3) Pull tight against the bundle of wood – that's it, the knot is complete.

Leave **no trace**

Most people interested in survival skills love the outdoors. They love the beauty and purity of the natural world, as well as using what nature provides for survival. If the outdoors is to stay beautiful and untouched, it is important that everyone who visits it treats it with respect. Always aim to leave each area just as you found it.

Everyone who uses the outdoors needs to work to keep it beautiful.

LITTER

Left-behind litter spoils the next person's visit, and is potentially harmful to animals. Always take litter home – especially glass, aluminium cans and foil, which will basically stay around forever. Burying litter is not a good idea: soil erosion can bring it to the surface, or animals may dig it up.

FIRES

When lighting a fire on grass, remove the turf and a few inches of soil so that the grass is not burned. Replace everything once the fire has gone out. In a wood, scrape away the leaf litter to prevent it drying out and lighting, causing a wildfire. Always put fires out by soaking the ground with water, then stirring it around so that no hot coals are left.

FYI!

Never light a fire on **peat**: it can smoulder underground for days, before starting a wildfire.

USING PLANTS AND TREES

Take only what you need! When picking a plant, don't always take it from the same area. Always try to leave roots intact, so that the plant can grow again. If the plant has a seed head, scatter the seeds around so replacements will grow. For wood, use dead wood where possible. If you do have to cut off a living branch, cut it flat across, close to the trunk, which gives the tree a better chance of surviving.

GOING TO THE TOILET

Never pee closer than 70 paces from water, and don't pee on a plant as it can damage or kill them. If you need to do more than a pee, dig a temporary toilet hole about knee deep. (Make sure the hole is at least 70 paces from any water sources.) When you have finished, fill in the hole.

FYI!

Pack out what you pack in – never leave *anything* behind in the wilderness.

pack out hiking expression meaning 'carry out' things you carry in
peat thick, dark soil that burns well when dried

Survival **food**

Water, not food, should be your first concern in a survival situation. You can survive for only three days without water, but three weeks without food! However, you will pretty soon be ravenously hungry – so once you have found a water source it will be time to think about what you can eat.

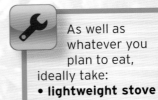

As well as whatever you plan to eat, ideally take:
• **lightweight stove**

CARRY YOUR OWN FOOD
Whenever you head off into the wild, take a little food with you. Bananas, muesli bars, cheese, nuts, dried fruit and filled rolls are all good for giving you a quick energy boost. On longer trips, take things that are light and will stay fresh. Crackers or pitta bread, for example, stay fresh longer than bread. If you don't want to carry a stove or flask, you can buy pre-made survival food packs. These contain a heating pouch that is set off when you add water.

WARNING!

Only **forage** for wild foods if you know for certain what is safe to eat. The results of eating a poisonous bug, plant or mushroom could be disastrous.

How hungry are you? Wood ants have a slightly lemony taste.

forage search for something, particularly food

FINDING WILD FOOD

Of course, you don't have to carry all your food with you. There are things you can eat growing all around you:

• Edible plants are easy to gather: at the right time of year there will be leaves you can eat everywhere.

• You may also be able to catch fish, rabbit, squirrel, pigeon, or pheasant. You might even be able to find some eggs! And if you're really hungry, how about some nice raw insects, such as ants? Or some cooked worms, frogs or snails?

Nettles can be made into a soup using hot water and salt. Pick the young leaves at the tip of the plant, these are the tastiest and freshest ones!

FYI!

Many insects are edible. Between 65–70% of an insect's body weight is protein, compared to 20–25% of most animals.

SECRET TRICK

One way to spice up a packet meal or some wild food is to add a bit of pepper and salt. You can carry these in specially made up straws:

1 Take a thick straw and cut it to length so it fits in your survival tin. Heat the end very gently until it becomes sticky, and squeeze it together with a pair of pliers.

2 Fill the straw with salt, pepper, or another spice. Leave enough empty so that you can gently heat the other end to seal it. Write what's inside on the side, and you're ready to go.

 Watch our expert feed himself in the wilderness, using only what's to hand! Check out the action at:
www.acblack.com/instantexpert

Life as a survival expert

If you can survive in the wild yourself, perhaps you could teach others to do the same?

This book has told you about the basic skills of survival: how to build a shelter, find safe drinking water and food, navigate your way in the wilderness, and signal for help if you are in trouble. For most people, being able to look after themselves in the wild is enough. But the very best survival experts make a living from their skills.

TEACHING SURVIVAL

In the last few years, an increasing number of survival courses have started up. People go on these to learn about shelter building, gathering wild food, **trapping**, navigation: all the skills you have read about in this book. As an instructor, you explain how things should be done, then watch everyone practising and point out ways they might be able to improve.

bushcraft wilderness skills
trapping catching wild animals

WORKING IN PUBLISHING

There are lots of websites, books, and magazines about survival skills and **bushcraft**. They all need writers, photographers, illustrators and designers who are interested in the subject. If you love to write (or design, or illustrate), this could be a way of putting your knowledge to good use.

TV WORK

The most famous survival and bushcraft experts - people like Bear Grylls and Ray Mears - are popular TV personalities. They spend their time developing their skills, filming, and coming up with ideas for new programmes. Of course, only a few people ever manage to get their own TV show! But if you work hard at your skills you *could* be the next Bear Grylls!

FYI!

Survival experts say: "The more you know, the less you carry." They mean that if you have knowledge of survival skills, you don't need to carry a lot of equipment.

Survival
troubleshooting

The skills needed to survive are simple, but sometimes things just don't seem as if they are working right. If you find yourself in a tricky or sticky situation, here are some top tips that might help you to put things right.

1. STAY CALM, AND USE "STOP"

Of course, any situation where you are trying to survive will be stressful. As well as the terrain, the weather, hunger and thirst, you may feel emotional stress. Loneliness, homesickness, doubt and fear can all combine to make it difficult to stay focused on the skills you need to survive. If you feel this panic coming over you, say to yourself: "STOP!"

S – Stop running about like a headless chicken! Identify the single most urgent problem you need to solve.

T – Think of how you can solve the problem.

O – Organize: once you have decided what to do, work out a plan of action.

P – Proceed: put your plan into action (but be flexible, you may have to make adjustments as you go).

2. FIRE LIGHTING IN THE WET

If you are struggling to get a fire started because it is damp or raining, try to build it somewhere dry, such as under a secure rock overhang. Other things you could try include:

a) Find some birch bark. This peels off the tree easily, and you can collect it in the wet. Because the bark is oily, it will light even when damp. Broken into thin strips it works really well with a fire steel, which works in the wet as well as in the dry.

b) If there are **conifers** close by, dead branches may be hanging or lying in the dry below the tree's thick foliage. Really dry branches will snap with a crack, and this **resinous wood** burns very well.

c) If the ground is damp, build a platform of sticks for your fire to sit on.

3. BOWDRILL BLUES

People often struggle to get a bowdrill working at first. If you find it tricky:

a) Find a long, reasonably thick pole and cut a notch in it, roughly in the centre. If you lash one end to a tree, you can use this as a lever to keep your drill in place with the right amount of pressure.

b) If there is more than one of you, Use a longer pole and work as a team. One can hold the pole while the other works the bow.

4. LEAKY DEBRIS SHELTER

If your debris shelter leaks, the chances are you need more debris! Pile it on until you have a good, deep layer. It is practically impossible to have too much – debris is very light, so it is unlikely to make your shelter collapse! This will not only solve the waterproofing, but also make your shelter warmer during the night.

FYI!

NEVER drink salt water without **desalinating** it!

5. WATER, WATER EVERYWHERE AND NOT A DROP TO DRINK!

If you find yourself stranded by the sea and there is no fresh water around, it is possible to **desalinate** salt water. This is a simple way to make seawater drinkable, if you have a stove with you:

a) fill a container with seawater and bring it to a rapid boil over a fire or stove.

b) place a clean piece of cloth (it can even be a corner torn off your T-shirt) over the top of the pan like a lid. Make sure it does not touch the salt water.

c) The steam will eventually cause the cloth to become soaked with moisture. If you wring out the water into a cup, you'll find it does not contain salt. (Always take great care wringing out the moisture, as steam is extremely hot.)

desalinate remove salt
conifer evergreen tree that produces seeds in the form of cones
resinous wood containing a sticky flammable substance, notably fir and pine

Technical survival
language

bearing the direction you need to travel

bushcraft wilderness skills

conifer evergreen tree that produces seeds in the form of cones

desalinate remove salt

deterioration progressively getting worse

diameter distance across a circle at its widest point

firesteel stick of metal that creates a shower of sparks when scraped

forage search for something, particularly food

gorge hook type of fish hook that catches in the fish's throat

green wood living or recently cut wood, which is damp inside

hypothermia lowered body temperature: severe hypothermia can lead to death

insulated wrapped up to stop heat escaping

kindling material that burns easily and can be used when starting a fire

merino breed of sheep with very soft wool

northern hemisphere the northern half of the earth

notch V-shaped cut on the surface of something

pack out hiking expression meaning 'carry out' things you carry in

peat thick, dark soil that burns well when dried

resinous wood containing a sticky flammable substance, notably fir and pine

scat animal excrement or poo

seasoned wood without internal moisture, which is dry and burns well

southern hemisphere the southern half of the earth

spork eating tool combining spoon, fork and knife in one

terrain the physical features of the ground or land

tinder material for starting a fire

trapping catching wild animals

vegetation still device for turning condensation into drinking water

wick draw away moisture

working end end of a rope used to tie a knot

Further information

REFERENCE BOOKS

The Wilderness Survival Guide
Joe O'Leary (Watkins, 2010)
Gives details of many of the practical
skills you need in the great outdoors.

Need to Know? Outdoor Survival
John Wiseman (HarperCollins, 2006)
Be prepared with all 'Lofty' Wiseman's
basic survival techniques.

Born Survivor Bear Grylls
(Channel 4 Books, 2007)
Survival techniques from the most
dangerous places on earth, by one of
TV's leading survival experts.

Outdoor Survival Handbook Ray Mears
(Ebury Press, 2001)
A guide to the resources and materials
available in the wild, and how to use them
for food, shelter, warmth and navigation.

The Natural Navigator Tristan Gooley
(Virgin Books, 2010)
All sorts of information to help you
find your way around using nature's
signposts, from the feel of a rock to the
appearance of the moon.

MAGAZINES

Bushcraft & Survival Skills
An excellent magazine covering all
aspects of bushcraft and survival, such
as wild food, camp craft, fire lighting,
tracking, wildlife and much more.

WEBSITES

www.bushcraftmagazine.com
The website of *Bushcraft & Survival Skills*
magazine.

www.bushcraftusa.com
This is a discussion forum for bushcraft
and survival skills.

www.beargrylls.com
For everything you ever wanted to know
about Bear Grylls.

www.azbushcraft.com
This site contains an excellent A-Z of
bushcraft and survival skills.

www.naturalbushcraft.co.uk
This site provides lots of free bushcraft
videos, articles, guides and more, from
kit-lists to how to make your own knife.

Survival timeline

247 BC
The first compass is invented in ancient China. (People will have to wait until the early 20th century for the liquid-filled magnetic compass we use today.)

Late 1800s
It is said that the Folgate Silver Plate Company produced a version of the spork in the late 1800s. Samuel W. Francis invented a combination spoon/fork/knife resembling the modern spork, which was patented in the US in 1874. The word 'spork' first appeared in dictionaries in 1909.

1907
The Scout organization is started by Robert Baden-Powell, with the aim of teaching survival and campcraft skills to boys. (Today it is open to boys and girls from the age of 6.)

1915-1916
Endurance, the ship of Antarctic explorer Ernest Henry Shackleton, is crushed in pack ice. The crew abandons the ship, and their aim became merely to survive. Shackleton leads the crew across the ice, then in lifeboats to a camp on Elephant Island. For six months most remain there and survive on seal meat and blubber. Shackleton and five others travel around the island to the north, then voyage across 1300km (800 miles) of treacherous ocean to South Georgia Island. He then hikes with two others across the island's uncharted interior to a whaling station, and summons a rescue party. The 22 men on Elephant Island are rescued on 30 August 1916, almost two years since their voyage began.

1959
John 'Lofty' Wiseman becomes the youngest person ever to be selected for the SAS at the age of 18 years. He serves with them for 26 years; in 1985, Wiseman releases *The SAS Survival Handbook*, which sparks increased interest in survival skills.

1972
In October 1972, a plane carrying a Uruguayan rugby team crashes in the Andes. The 16 passengers left alive resort to extreme survival behaviour, eating the frozen meat of those killed in the crash. All 16 remaining passengers survive, and are rescued on December 23, 1972, more than two months after the plane crashed.

1976
Gore-Tex is co-invented by Wilbert L. Gore, Rowena Taylor, and Gore's son Robert W. Gore. It is a new fabric that keeps people dry in wet weather, but does not get sweaty during high-energy activities such as hiking. Gore-Tex and similar fabrics have revolutionized outdoor clothing, making it more efficient and comfortable than ever before.

1987
Mors Kochanski, a world-famous wilderness skills instructor based in Canada, helps popularize the term 'bushcraft' in his book *Northern Bushcraft*, (re-released in 1998 titled *Bushcraft*).

1998
Bear Grylls becomes the youngest person to have climbed Everest. He later becomes a TV personality and presenter of survival shows.

2003
In Blue John Canyon, Utah, USA, hiker and climber Aron Ralston's arm becomes trapped when a giant boulder pins it against a canyon wall. Five days later he cuts off his arm using a blunt knife. He is found by hikers, then rescued by a helicopter, and survives.

2004
Les Stroud creates, writes, films and edits the 'Survivorman' TV series. Audiences respond well to the sight of Les surviving in remote locations, with no support team or camera crew, and the series is a hit.

1990
British bushcraft and survival expert Ray Mears releases *The Survival Handbook*. He becomes a presenter of TV programmes about bushcraft and survival, and later publishes several other books on the subject.

Index